He Still Sings Over Me

BY CATHEY DANIEL

POEMS TOUCHED BY THE FATHER'S GRACE, VOLUME 2

He Still Sings Over Me

BY CATHEY DANIEL

POEMS TOUCHED BY THE FATHER'S GRACE, VOLUME 2

He Still Sings Over Me
POEMS TOUCHED BY THE FATHER'S GRACE, VOLUME 2

Copyright © 2020 By Cathey Daniel

ISBN 978-0-9764325-5-5

All rights reserved. No part of this book may be reproduced or utilized in any form or by any means, electronic or mechanical, including photocopying or recording, by any information or retrieval system, without written permission from the author.

Published by **Oil Tree Publishers,** Edmond, Oklahoma
A division of WildHorse Consulting, LLC | wildhorsebiz.com
Printed in the U.S.A.

Cover and interior design: Laura Marshall Clark.
Cover photos courtesy of Jason Duane Luman.
Interior photos courtesy of Jason Duane Luman and Cindy Daniel.

For more information about this book or Cathey Daniel's first volume of poetry, *As He Sings Over Me,* email: jadced@yahoo.com.

Acknowledgments

This author is indebted to many who have encouraged me to write this book. First of all, I am indebted to my heavenly Father who sings over me; and then, to my earthly family: husband Olene, sons John Allen and Justin, daughters-in-law Cindy and Kristie, and seven beautiful grandchildren who are and continue to be a blessing and an inspiration.

Many thanks to Laura Marshall Clark for her friendship, support, assistance with and design of this book, and to Jason Luman for his generous permission to include his stunning photography.

There are many friends and co-workers through the years who have encouraged me to publish my work. Although they are too many to mention here, I am genuinely thankful for their encouragement.

Table of Contents

	Foreword	ix
	Introduction	x
	"The Promise"	xiii
Chapter 1	The Family	15
Chapter 2	Those We Hold Dear	21
Chapter 3	Times & Seasons	33
Chapter 4	Drawn to His Presence	45
Chapter 5	The Lighter Side	65
Chapter 6	Beholding Beauty	75

Foreword

She opens her mouth with wisdom, and on her tongue is the law of kindness. She watches over the ways of her household, and does not eat the bread of idleness. Her children rise up and call her blessed; Her husband also, and he praises her. Many daughters have done well, but you excel them all. Charm is deceitful and beauty is passing, but a woman who fears the Lord, she shall be praised.

Proverbs 31:26-30 (NKJV)

The scripture above from Proverbs describes Cathey Daniel. Her nature is kind, compassionate, quiet, while at the same time, fierce. When she speaks, be ready—there is wisdom coming. She is a source of beauty, wisdom, encouragement, and peace.

This book is a collection of poetry that Cathey has written. As you read, let the peace of God that exudes from the author wash over you. Cathey's words will inspire you to creativity, will encourage you, will comfort you, and will give you morsels of wisdom.

Relax and position yourself for a journey.

Roy and Michelle Vanderburg
Pastors—The Family, Atoka, Oklahoma

Introduction

When I published my first poetry book, *As He Sings Over Me,* I wrote an introduction as real to me today as it was when I lived it as a young girl. I include it again in this second collection of poetry to honor a lifelong work of God in my life, and to thank Him once more for who He designed me to be.

The love of poetry began when I was a small child, and my daddy was responsible for my love affair with poetry. He was tall with dark hair and eyes, broad shoulders, and a deep voice. Although he never completed college, he was very intelligent and mechanically inclined. He seemed to be able to fix anything that was broken, from a record player to the car.

Often at night I would listen to Daddy quote poetry. This would begin after he had a couple of stout drinks. He would lean against the kitchen counter or pace the floor and announce:

> "There are strange things done in the midnight sun
> By the men who moil for gold;
> The Arctic trails have their secret tales
> That would make your blood run cold;
> The Northern Lights have seen queer sights,
> But the queerest they ever did see
> Was that night on the marge of Lake Lebarge
> I cremated Sam McGee."

He memorized short poems and long poems which told a story, like *The Cremation of Sam McGee,* by Robert Service. I loved the sound of rhyming words and alliteration as his voice rose and fell in the telling of those poems. That love of stories and sound has followed me all my life. I now believe that God was preparing me to reach out into the field of poetry.

At the age of seven or eight I began to write my own poetry. Mother often had to call me to supper several times while the words came tumbling across the page. Many times the paper and pencil went to the supper table with me because I could not stop writing.

God has used the gift of prophecy through His messengers in the Body of Christ to encourage and exhort me in this creative gift of poetry. The Lord impressed them to tell me that when I write, God Himself sings over me. Different individuals have shared spiritual insight that God sings over me when I write, although they neither knew the others who have spoken to me, nor the identical words that others gave me. For this reason, I have entitled this book: *He Still Sings Over Me* from Zephaniah 3:17 (KJV).

Often when I sit down to write, I can actually sense His presence and I know that He sings over me. The complete verse says:

The Lord thy God in the midst of thee is mighty;
He will save, He will rejoice over thee with joy;
He will rest in His love,
He will joy over thee with singing.

God has been singing over me for a long time, and I give Him all the credit for what He has written through me. Sometimes I experience difficulty in expressing verbally what is in my heart, but when I release it to God, it often comes out in poetry form.

As you read this book, I pray you will be blessed, and that God will receive the glory for what He has done through me.

The Promise

What can I type? I really don't know
God, you promised me that you would show
You prophesied to me with earnest zest
The book that I wrote would be the best

So here I sit and I start to age
Staring solemnly at a very blank page
Writing a book is not an easy task
You said I could do it. Now why do I ask?

You'd think an idea would pop into view
I have no idea so I'm trusting in you
I hope that I haven't waited too long
Missing your timing, now that would be wrong

It won't be too difficult for me you said
But all the while I have waited in dread
You promised a download sent forth in love
The words would land on me like a dove

I'm waiting, I'm watching. Please don't let it be
That you've changed your mind and some other will see
The book you were planning to write through my pen
Lord, give me a chance to write once again

God, sing over me as you did times before
And show me the book that you are longing for
I'll lay that job down if that's your desire
I can't do it alone. You must inspire

I'll praise you and thank you. Worship I'll bring
I honor you Jesus, my Savior and King
I position myself with trust in my heart
That you'll show me the place you want me to start

That it will go to the nations I trust to be true
For the story I write will be coming from you
My computer is ready and I'm ready now
I'll give it my best if you'll just show me how

Chapter 1

The Family

Family Generations

Family begins with a husband and wife
  Agreed and committed to each other for life
  Many trials they work through learning to adjust
  In lots of situations they simply learn to trust
  Love brings the children, precious girls and boys
  Young hearts bring new issues, new insights and joys

Children are blessings from heaven above
  Happy little people full of mischief and love
  In a loving environment they grow up to be
  Like their parents, they must strive to agree
  Days go by swiftly and childhood soon passes
  Remembering friends and tough high school classes
  Even college swiftly flies as they continue to date
  Now the time has come they are looking for a mate

Great is their love and commitment for life
  Ready and eager as husband and wife
  Anxious to be parents and follow the crowd
  Now it is time to make grandparents proud
  Days pass slowly especially for Grands
  Can't wait to hold tiny ones again in their hands
  Happiness spreads as the family grows
  Increasing in more wiggly fingers and toes
  Love watching them grow and experience life
  Don't want them to suffer or see them have strife
  Really we're not ready to face the next page
  Excitement is diminished as we face old age
  Now Lord, continue to bless and increase
      and may all of them follow You.

This poem was written for my husband, Olene, after attending a "Women's Respect" Dare meeting. It was suggested that we try to find a knight statue to give to our husband, letting him know that he is our Knight in Shining Armor.

My Knight

There's something very special that I wanted you to know.
Something I could tell you, and something I could show.

I prayed before the trip that God would grant for me to find
A Knight in Shining Armor that I pictured in my mind.

I searched in vain in every place wherever we would shop.
It seemed like a futile effort, but I determined not to stop.

It was there in Lindsborg, Kansas, that God answered my prayer.
As I walked into that tiny shop I saw him sitting there.

It's just a simple reminder as a gift to you from me.
You're MY Knight in Shining Armor for all the world to see.

You've been my lover, my protector, my provider, and a friend.
For fifty years you've been faithful, for on you I can depend.

I simply want to honor you for all that you have done
To make my life and marriage a very happy one!

The Daniel Tree

Our seven precious grandchildren are beautiful in every way.

Yet each and every child is so different. Bless them Lord, I pray.

I declare they hunger for Your Word. They each are students of prayer.

Their tender hearts beat with compassion. They are always willing to share.

Their character is without question for they walk in integrity.

Miracles, signs, and wonders follow them as they walk in authority.

Their gifts and callings are different, but in dreams and visions I see

They are being used in the Kingdom. God has called them to ministry.

They are arrows in the hand of their father and each will find his/her mark.

They are beacons set upon a hill bringing beautiful light out of dark.

They are righteous seeds that are growing and each the Lord will bless.

For they are tiny acorns becoming great Oaks of Righteousness.

Nathaniel Westin

Kaitlyn Anne

Samuel James

Ruth Elizabeth

Jacob Ray

Joseph Washington

Benjamin John

Destin, Florida 2014

We came from Oklahoma in a van filled to the brim
To the beautiful state of Florida to relax, have fun, and swim

It took us twenty hours with pit stops along the way
With four adults and five children determined to relax and play

We arrived at our destination where anxiety and wonder blends
What will this condo be like, this place they call Sea Winds?

What a pleasant surprise we encountered, so grateful and blessed
A beautiful home away from home, a haven of comfort and rest

There's nothing quite so wonderful than to play in surf and sand
To experience God's creation so mighty, majestic and grand

On the beach were artistic people with simply some sand and a pail
We created an alligator. They made a shark, turtle, and whale

We love the sound of the ocean as it gently rolls to the beach
Its continuous sound is soothing. It fills our hearts with such peace

To sit on the deck and read, to me, is truly a special pleasure
Those quiet moments to meditate are times I certainly treasure

Thank you for letting us share your home for such a little while
The memories are ever so precious. To remember makes us smile

We all agree. We love Sea Winds #3

The Daniel Family

Chapter 2

Those We Hold Dear

A Feather of Revelation

Sometimes visiting grandsons make requests
as they spend the night with grandparents as guests.
When Ben, our youngest grandson, was only three
He curiously came and asked this question of me.

"Do you have any stuffed toys I can play with?" he said.
"I brought two to sleep with when we go to bed."
A thoughtful, puzzled look crawled across my face.
I couldn't recall a single stuffed toy left at our place.

For the past twenty years I had taught in Pre-K,
but most of those things had been given away.
In my classroom we had crafted a huge paper tree.
Sitting up on a branch perched a little monkey.

With a long curly tail and a cute little face,
I hoped I had kept him and put him up some place.
In the den on the bookshelf I happened to see
that sweet little monkey just staring at me.

I said, "Will this little monkey be okay with you?"
The look on his face was too good to be true.
The humongous grin and the shine in his eyes
was a wonderful picture of total surprise!

"His name is Coco. He doesn't like to be alone.
If you would like to, you may take him home."
With a giant hug he then came running my way.
I thought he was ready to sit down and play.

He hurried to his backpack and was busy for a minute.
I thought that he was going to put the monkey in it.
But instead he said, "Here is a feather I'm giving to you."
The reason he was giving it to me I had no clue.

"My daddy gave me this feather, and I give it to you for free.
You gave me that monkey, now you have something from me."
"But don't you want to keep it since it came from your dad?"
"But I want you to have it. That will make me glad."

My heart melted in love as I placed the feather on the shelf.
I knew he was thinking of others, and not only about himself.
What a beautiful revelation came to me out of the blue.
The Word says give to others and others will give to you.

Give, and it shall be given unto you; good measure, pressed down and shaken together, and running over, shall men give unto your bosom. For with the same measure that ye mete withal it shall be measured to you again.

Luke 6:38

To the Bus Driver

There's a special brand of people who stand out from all of us
They are called to transport children on the yellow school bus
They rise up early morning and they rush to take their place
With earnest, fervent prayer they ask for mercy and for grace

This year the children are different and yet they are the same
For life is just a party and going to school is just a game
But serious are the drivers and safety is their goal
For they carry beautiful children and precious is each soul

To transport a group of children requires skill without doubt
For distractions come in multitudes within the bus and out
Talking, laughing, and squealing lift noise up to a roar
Wiggling, jostling children grab books dropped on the floor

The driver checks his mirror keeping children in his sight
In hopes that a simple argument does not erupt in fight
As busy becomes the traffic and travel slows to a crawl
Back in the bus there's disturbance. A little one starts to bawl

As traffic begins to move again there's tension etched in his face
He remembers his morning prayer and thanks God again for His grace
He delivers his cargo safely and drops them off with a grin
But time is short and he must report to bring them back home again

He savors the sudden quiet. There's naught but the motor's groan
For sweet is the sound of silence. What peace just to be alone
We often take for granted those who exert such concern
In taking our precious children to the places where they can learn

As you travel the busy streets and roads with caution and gentle care
Know that God hears and answers your earnest and fervent prayer
Thank you for being a servant and taking the load off of us
We appreciate your service in driving the yellow school bus

The Mourning Man

It's 3:00 a.m. and I can't sleep
I look out the window and want to weep

There are lights in the window in the house up ahead
A man is in mourning and can't sleep in his bed

Cancer took its toll and the man lost his wife
Now heartache and regret are tugging at his life

I don't know what it's like for one to lose a spouse
But I can imagine the silence in an empty house

Loneliness is torture and the voices start to come
I should have, and wish I had, and things I could have done

It takes a lot of time to heal and overcome the grief
At first it seems there is no way to give the soul relief

But life goes on and one must choose to release the grief and pain
Make an honest effort to embrace life once again

I pray for the man who has lost his precious wife
That even in her death, his choice will be life

The Intercessor

She sees in a vision the blood on her hands
But why does she see it? She can't understand
She's a prayer warrior who has gone to the unknown
On God's motorcycle with speed and hair full-blown

With prayer and intercession she has captured God's heart
God is sending her to places that have been literally blown apart
Who knows? It may be to Israel, to Yemen, or Afghanistan
God is sending her to minister, thus the blood is on her hands

In the midst of suffering and pain, she simply chose to be
Closer to the Father in prayer and sweet intimacy
She's being transported in the night – an intercessor on the go
To minister to others that she doesn't even know

Great is her calling as she ministers to those in need
I pray God's blessings over her. Give her motorcycle speed
She will not need a helmet to calm her flying hair
It's proof she's on assignment. Only God can get her there

To the Nursery Workers at Church

To some very special people that we couldn't do without
Who rescue us so many times and help us without doubt
You give your time as servants and often without pay
Your work is never easy even though it looks like play

Thank you, nursery workers, for sharing of your time
So we could sit in service and soak up every line
Thanks for rocking babies – for drying all their tears
For telling them of Jesus and comforting their fears

Thanks for taking them to potty and cleaning up the poop
And feeding them a snack as they gather in a group
For teaching them to worship and praise the Lord in song
To share and say, "I'm sorry," when a little one does wrong

"Suffer the children and forbid them not," I heard the Master say
That is what you do for them as you teach them day by day
God calls his most anointed to the Nursery to serve in love
For children are most precious to the Heavenly Father above

Don't think that others don't notice all that you do and care
For giving your life for others by being so willing to share
Your service and undying labor of love we appreciate
We sincerely give you honor for you are simply GREAT!

Food for Thought

The old man slowly shuffled into the quiet room
At the Food Storehouse where I worked one late afternoon
"May I help you?" I said. "Have you been here before?"
He shook his head no with his eyes to the floor

"Please fill this out," I said and handed him paper and pen
He refused to even look at me and shook his head again
"Sir, would you like to sit down and fill the paper out?"
He seemed to be in fear as he slowly looked about

His eyes lit on a table and I knew he wanted to sit down
I followed him with paper and pen trying not to frown
"I came here to get some food, but that's not all I need…
Will you fill it out?" he softly asked. "I don't know how to read."

As I looked into his eyes they filled with tears of shame
"I'll gladly help you all I can. Please tell me your name."
I learned the man was eighty-two. He had worked hard all his life
He had never learned to read and just depended on his wife

Now she was gone, he was alone, and needed food for the table
But jobs were few and at eighty-two he found he was not able
"We'll get you food to last this month and more if there is a need…
And I can help you even more. I can teach you how to read.

If you will come in here once a week and give me an hour or so
I can teach you how to read and then you will really grow."
He shook his head and sadly said, "The idea is really great
But thank you, no. I won't come because it is way too late."

"It's never too late to learn to read. It won't cost a single dime.
If you have the will, I have the skill, it just takes a little time."
Nothing I said convinced him that reading could better his fate
He refused food to feed his mind, but accepted food for his plate

He went to the door and said, "Thank you for meeting my basic need."
"You're welcome," I said, but deep inside my heart greatly grieved
Once out the door he turned to the west. I never saw him again
Refusing to risk and choosing to live with only what might have been

Tonight as I read to my grandson, my heart was filled with joy
Thank you, God, for the privilege of reading to this little boy
It made me think of the old man who thought it was way too late
Reading is a privilege and honor and a gift to appreciate

•

The Nest

There was a beautiful mother bird who labored at her nest
For soon there would be little ones. She wanted for them the best
She built her nest high in the tree where they would be safe and sound
No predators would bother them who stalked upon the ground
When spring rains came the wind was fierce and every day it blew
Until the branch lost all its strength and simply broke in two
Down came the nest and the tiny eggs, which broke in the terrible fall
Mother bird wept with pain when she saw that she had lost them all
As spring came again her wisdom grew and she already made her plan
For she was watching the old rusty tractor and observing the little man
The tractor stood still day after day except for once in a while
The little old man would crank it up and go down the road with a smile
Then late in the evening he'd bring it back and park in the very same place
He'd take off his cap and head for the house still with a smile on his face
Mother bird studied little man's face and found it to be soft and tender
So she built her nest in the safest place on the tractor's rusty fender
She laid her eggs and took a rest, and soon her babies arrived
The little man came and smiled again, glad that they had survived
Busy days were in store for her as she flew both north and south
It was all she could do to find the food for each hungry open mouth
One fine day the little man came and took the tractor away
But mother bird knew he would be back at the end of his busy day
She gathered food for her little ones then waited in quiet trust
For the man would bring her babies home. He always came back at dusk
As the little man brought the tractor back into its special place
Mother bird flew to meet him and noticed the smile on his face
God watches over His creation and He has a special plan
God's eye is on the sparrow, but He places His heart in the man
I'm sure there's a place of honor in the Hall of Fame where God names
Those special people who carry His heart like that of Carl 'Sock' James

The Nest was written in memory of Carl 'Sock' James who truly was the man with a heart after his God and loved every one of His creatures. Photo courtesy of Cindy Daniel.

Chapter 3

Times & Seasons

The Pumpkin on the Porch

A funny thing happened at our school. I'm sure you will agree

It's almost unbelievable. I wish you could have come to see

It happened the end of October when the days were nice and cool

I brought a big fat pumpkin to share with my Pre-K class at school

We cut the top off of it and each child scooped I confess

For strings and seeds landed everywhere. It really was a mess

We washed the seeds and fried them to make a tasty snack

Then we drew a very funny face decorating both front and back

It sat in our class for several days on a shelf in the very same spot

But after a while it began to shrink and the insides were black with rot

At last the pumpkin began to smell. It was time to throw it away

So I went to the porch of our building and pitched it at the end of the day

"It's the end of that," I said to myself as it burst in the grass still green

Our beautiful pumpkin was nothing but mush as it smashed to smithereen

With never another thought of it, I daily went on about teaching

But deep in the soil seeds met death and new life began its reaching

Spring came and went and the children too as we took a break from school

But soft in its bed new life lay ahead in the earth that was moist and cool

The sun shone bright, soft winds blew, and the earth was blessed with rain

And I found myself in the middle of summer preparing to teach again

As I entered the building my eyes beheld a bountiful growth of green

Leaves and vines all intertwined growing strong now could be seen

The twisted vines grew up the fence that surrounded the brick-red porch

Healthy green like you've never seen in spite of the sun's hot scorch

Deep in the vines you could clearly see several blooms of brilliant gold

The promise of new little pumpkins was a beautiful sight to behold

From the death of a seed God did indeed bring forth life on the healthy vine

Right in the corner of the Pre-K porch we witnessed a miracle divine

Only God can bring a sweet gentle rain or a kiss from the summer heat

And bring eternal seed out of death in a grave and call the fruit of it sweet

God's Plan for Celebration

As autumn's presence fills the air I pause and then reflect
How soon the chill of winter's cold will swiftly interject
It's barely into September when Christmas signs appear
Beautiful ornaments, trees and lights, and carols ring out cheer

October then begins for all with little time for thanks
We are overcome by Halloween, with all its tricks and pranks
Beautiful fall colors fill the landscape ever bright
But everything from costumes to shows fill the air with fright

November brings Thanksgiving with food that tastes amazing
Everyone is filling up like cattle slowly grazing
We stuff our mouths with turkey and delicious pumpkin pie
We're miserable as we can be and even wonder why

We rush from the family table. Our minds refuse to stop
Can't wait to hit the streets because it's time for us to shop
And then the rush is on to buy in frantic disarray
Everything we see and want that's open for display

Commercialism has become our gift from the enemy's hand
And we have forgotten it is God who has a more perfect plan
Jesus, God's only begotten Son, is our soul entire reason
To thank the Father for His love and celebrate the season

He's waiting for you each morning, to listen and then to pray
His presence will go with you through each step along the way
Don't let Christmas become controlled by the enemy's ugly hand
Set your goal as a prosperous soul and stick to the Father's plan

On a Dark Day

Where do you want me? What must I do?
I'm having difficulty just trusting you!
Many times I question, am I really saved?
Did I blow my chances? Have I been enslaved?

Am I walking in deception? Can I not see clear?
My ears are open, but am I able to hear?
I fear I'm in the wilderness just wandering around,
That I've missed you completely and I never will be found.

Lord, take my doubt and unbelief. Just fill me with your hope.
I really want to walk with you. I'm tired of trying to cope.
I see the others going on, but I have lost my purse.
Am I dying in the wilderness living out a curse?

To walk in the Spirit is my desire, to clearly hear from the throne.
To know you will never forsake me, and that I'm not doing this alone.
I long to walk in your favor and be one of whom you are proud,
So if my identity's stolen, that is something that you have allowed.

Whatever may be my future upon you only can I depend.
I pray for the privilege of being one whom you call faithful friend.
Forgive me for always missing the mark, for being slow to obey.
Allow repentance to grip my heart. Show me the narrow way.

A Christmas to Remember

A Christmas worth remembering is not about you and me

It's not about the gifts piled high under the Christmas tree

It's not about decorations or carols sung by a choir

Not about chestnuts roasting on an open roaring fire

It's not about a man in red or reindeer and a sleigh

It's not about children laughing or acting in a play

It's not about a single thing that has been created by man

It's all about a mighty God and His awesome unique plan

For God desired fellowship and intimacy with you and me

That's why He gave His only Son, plan A. There's no plan B

The greatest gift given came from God when He gave His only Son

Before the foundation of the world His love for us had begun

He calls us to simply trust in Him and in His name believe

Salvation, deliverance, and healing are blessings we then receive

To make His name glorious was the reason for our creation

And to spread the Kingdom of God in love to each and every nation

When we consider the sacrifice God made just for you and me

We can't help but come to Him thankfully with deepest intimacy

Thank God for the veil that was rent in two so we can boldly converse

And share our hearts and hear the voice of the God of the Universe

Now is the time to move at His sound out of our comfortable pew

Into the seven mountains and do what we're called to do

Awaken your hearts to the message of what God has already done

Don't wait to hear the Father say, "I called, but you didn't come."

The harvest is right in front of us. Just take a look at your field

We are laborers unto the harvest, we simply have to yield

A Mall Moment

While shopping at the mall I happened to meet
A very nice gentleman when I stopped to eat

He asked to sit down at my table for a bit
The food court was full and nowhere else to sit

He had a kind face and a very pleasant smile
I welcomed him to join me at the table for a while

Polite conversation was all that took place
But I felt a little uneasy as he stared at my face

"It's getting quite late and time for me to go,"
As I rose up from my chair he simply said, "No!

I've something to tell you that you need to hear
You're a very rich person. More rich than you appear."

I sat down once again and I declared, "That is so,
I am so much richer than you will ever know

My Father owns the cattle on every hill and more
He owns every drop of water that washes on the shore

Because I am His daughter His love for me abounds
I'm forever grateful and praise to Him resounds

He sent His Son to die for me who willingly took my place
So I could live in health and wealth covered by His grace."

"What you have said is very true, but there is so much more
So I was sent to share with you what stands behind a door

It's a door of simple entitlement with others that you share
It's all about you, how you're blessed, but others are not there

The world is screaming out for help. They don't know what to do
You're standing here with the answers, but you just enjoy the view

I know you are His child my dear, but I need for you to see
There's so much more that you can do simply by decree

So open your mouth, release the sound as revelation thunders
It's time my child so speak it loud, Miracles, Signs, and Wonders

You are Jesus walking on the earth. You carry His DNA
Do not worry. It's not your job. He only asks you to pray

Pray and declare and be a word to others God brings your way
That is the simple message God is giving to you today."

I thanked the man for obedience in giving the message to me,
But I think the message is for all of us. I'm hoping you will agree.

A Prosperous Soul

I looked at my house with intensity as I was cleaning today
The things I am doing are the very things I did just yesterday
My dining room table is cluttered with mail I gave only a glance
Intending to read it more carefully if ever I got the chance

Several bills are in a stack with two which are overdue
Amidst the several catalogs waiting for me to look through
Daily newspapers across the couch and a few dropped on the floor
Yesterday tennis shoes and a pair of socks hastily slung by the door

A skillet and pans left on the stove and dirty dishes left in the sink
They make me aware of their presence as I encounter the stink
Glasses and cups are in several rooms where I left them yesterday
Too busy with doing other things, I failed to put them away

Several outfits lay on the bed from trying to decide what to wear
Some were clean, some were dirty, and others in need of repair
Dirty laundry stacked in the hall, and more on the bathroom floor
I wash, dry, and put them away so I can wash them once more

A den in our house is disaster and is controlled by the clutter king
My husband is known for bringing and stashing almost anything
Fingernail clippers and flashlights, horse blankets and various tools
Boots with stirrups, shotgun shells, sale bills for cattle and mules

Closets are basically hidey holes because you can shut the door
And no one can see all the clothes and the stuff lying on the floor
I see why people rent storage units to keep all their extra stuff
If I built a larger house to fill, the extra space wouldn't be enough

It's time to have a garage sale and get rid of things I don't need
Like ceramics, boxes of whatnots, and books I will never read
Clothes that I love, but I can't wear, shoes that are way out of style
Various papers from who knows where stuck in an old worn file

Junk in the buffet and under the beds, drawers filled up to the top
Why do we try to keep everything? It's time to simply say STOP
It comes from a poverty spirit which daily grows out of control
God's commanded blessing is to live from a prosperous soul

I shudder to think that when I die that others would come to know
All the things that I held on to were things that I needed to let go
There's nothing I can take with me, so why try to keep it now
Lord, help me get my life in control. I trust you to show me how

Guide with wisdom and knowledge from the Word on angel wings
Deliver me from lusting and loving the possession of earthly things
To be a trustworthy steward of all you have placed in my hand
Is my ultimate goal and desire, and to complete what you command

Chapter 4

Drawn to His Presence

Morning Prayer

Dear Father, I have a desire to share
I just want you to show me where

I'm totally blessed and ready to give
So others can receive and even live

Open my eyes to see the need
In obedience I will plant the seed

Be it a word, a gift or even cash
Help me respond in just a flash

Mentor Me

God delivered to me a gentle reminder

That I was in need of a good pathfinder

I thought for a moment and knew it was true

My greatest desire is that it be you

Would you consider? How nice it would be

That you could speak life and direction to me

Look with discernment and let His light shine

On the little foxes that have spoiled the vine

Speak words of wisdom and help me draw near

Into His presence – that place I hold dear

Dreaming Again

I'm dreaming again but just don't know what the dream

could mean.

Each has a different topic, and each has a different scene.

I know that God is talking, but the message does not seem clear.

I can't understand the picture. Perhaps I interpret with fear.

I know God wants me to understand and search to find a way

To realize what He's saying so then I can obey.

I pray He will grant me wisdom and the ability to discern

What His desire is for me, and what I still need to learn.

My identity has been determined. He wants to identify me,

But I can only receive it, through Him in intimacy.

That's where I've failed and missed it. I've made it all about pride,

And that's why a hollow and empty place seems in me to reside.

Holy Spirit, help me to spend time in His presence again,

To conquer this giant of running with fear, to overcome pride

and just win!

I Am a Book

I am a dusty little book sitting high upon a shelf

Afraid to be pulled out and read for it's all about myself

But destiny demands it and that I cannot deny

God said He will meet me in it if I will only try

Obedience requires sacrifice so I must pull away

To listen to His heartbeat, His words to me and pray

In the wee hours of the morning I silently wait and wonder

To experience His presence – to hear His voice of thunder

As I focus on His goodness and promises He has made

Those clinging thoughts of doubt and fear soon begin to fade

Truth replaces deceitful lies and freedom starts to reign

He brings release to hidden anger, bitterness, and pain

His presence hovers over me. I hear Him sweetly sing

He reminds me I am Royalty and the daughter of a King

I can do all things through Christ so you can plainly see

This small book is written by God in, on, and through me

Habitation

Jesus, I just want to come and sit down at your feet

To experience your presence in fellowship sweet

I want to hear you whisper that you love me once again

That I'm your favorite daughter and you also call me friend

I want to worship you once more all my praise repeat

I long to sit upon your lap and feel your heart's steady beat

I want to tell you thanks a lot for all that you have done

For giving me the strength to run the race I have to run

I don't want a one-time encounter or a simple visitation

But I desire a daily and a frequent habitation

Lord Jesus, you abide with me as I abide with you

And I will be obedient to do the things you tell me to

joy

Tell me if you've seen her. I'm always looking out for joy.

She's not a game or festival. She's certainly not a toy.

They say that she's inside of me, but I cannot get her out.

I'm told she's in there somewhere, but I begin to doubt.

Did I lose her in my childhood when I was in despair?

I really can't remember her ever being there.

Happy moments from the past flash across my mind

But joy just seems to be remiss within my own design.

They say joy comes in the morning but I've never met her there

I remember pain and sorrow and things that were not fair

I've seen joy in other people, but I cannot find her in my heart

She's like a missing piece of puzzle before you even start

I've looked for her in places, in friends, and simple things

I've looked for her in things to buy like furniture and rings

Maybe she was stolen by the enemy who lies

That would be just like him. His tactics are no surprise

I decided just to ask a friend, "Where did you get your joy?"

"Not from places or things," she said. "Not from a girl or a boy..."

Joy is something that comes to you as part of God's unique plan

The moment you are introduced to a very special man

As you hear what Jesus has done for you and in your heart believe

By placing your trust in Jesus and the Word, you then can receive

Inheritance is there for the taking as you become daughter or son

Who lives to extend the Kingdom to each and every one

As our mind becomes renewed to the Spirit of Truth and His love

Joy unspeakable full of glory comes to dwell in you from above

Joy is a promise given to you so receive the revelation

Rejoice and be exceedingly glad. Proclaim with celebration

By putting Jesus first in your life, then Other's needs are cast

The Y in joy represents Yourself, putting yourself last

Jesus first
Others second
Yourself last

Jesus has been made to me: righteousness, peace, and joy.

The Doctor

I had an appointment with the doctor trying hard not to be late
It was an examination, the kind of which I hate
They handed me a gown and sheet and left me standing there
In an old examination room shivering cold and bare

I sat for such a long time, overcome with dread
Sometimes it's even harder when you know what lies ahead
It sounded like a party was going on out in the hall
Doctor and nurses were laughing, having themselves a ball

I was starting to feel abandoned so I began to pray
I asked the Lord, "Give me grace to face this thing today."
Then I remembered Jesus how He suffered on a tree
That every bit of punishment He took was just for me

I had been complaining in the midst of all my wealth
Suffering a small discomfort so I could walk in health
"Thank you Lord for all you've done," was all that I could pray
Then a mighty ton of dread and fear was lifted off that day

The exam was swiftly completed and in a very short while
I left the doctor's office wearing a knowing smile
That God is always faithful when you go through thick or thin
He's constantly aware of every fix you've gotten in

Provision from the Father already has been made
So step into the situation and just 'Do it afraid!'
Trust Him with your every care for nothing is too small
It thrills the Father's heart to hear His precious children call

Trust

Taking every thought captive to the obedience of Jesus Christ

Refusing to do my own thing or spout my own opinions

Understanding that apart from Him I can do nothing

Staying connected daily in relationship through prayer and the Word

Thanksgiving and praise through every circumstance regardless whether it is good or bad

Trust is a Must

    Refuse to Abuse

        Understand it's not about me, but Him

            Stay in relationship every day

                Thank and praise for He is the way

Plow Deep

God has clearly spoken to go deeper with the plow
We want to obey Him but say we don't know how
The plow is a vital instrument we have within our hands
Part of it is giving to the Father the honor He demands

We can give Him thanksgiving for all that He has done
Praise Him for His love and the wonderful things to come
Worship Him with abandonment for the great I Am is He
Then wait upon His presence to experience His glory

Our hands and lips move the plow to go deeper into the sod
With thanksgiving, praise, worship, and glory we magnify God
Singing, shouting, clapping, dancing, waving our arms in the air
Relishing His presence as we spend time with Him in prayer

Whatsoever a man sows, the Word says he also will reap
Spending time with the Shepherd is a wise choice for His sheep
He has spoken to us in prophecy. He's given instructions for now
Let's give him our lips and our hands and go deeper with the plow

We just Want to be Faithful

We don't want to tease you, Lord
We don't want to just be playful
We just want to please you, Lord
We just want to be faithful

Giving you just a moment or two
Will never satisfy
You gave your everything to us
You sent your Son to die

You've given us your mighty Word
And asked us Lord to feast
To give it more than just a moment or two
To fill and then release

We don't want to tease you, Lord
We don't want to just be playful
We just want to please you, Lord
We just want to be faithful

You've called us into intimacy
You ask us just to believe
To place our trust completely in you
And then stand to receive

You've given us a measure of faith
A gift from your own store
Lord, multiply and make it grand
To serve you more and more

We don't want to tease you, Lord
We don't want to just be playful
We just want to please you, Lord
We just want to be faithful

The Inevitable

I really dread tomorrow, especially the lunch
For I will be having dinner with a very critical bunch

There will be griping and complaining that is so difficult to ignore
The very negative atmosphere will hit just inside the door

There will be sarcastic comments and gossip to the skies
All the things I hate the most and utterly despise

But I find myself caught up and doing just the same
Before I even know it, I'm putting down a name

Arguments come easily concerning politics and such
Everyone has his own opinion. It really is too much

Lord, help me keep my mouth shut and in my heart just pray
If they ask for my opinion, I'll say, "My, what a beautiful day!"

It suddenly crossed my mind that the problem may be ME
If that's the case, I repent. Lord give me eyes to see

Help me to be a model of love and thankfulness
Let the negative turn positive. Let my mouth only bless

You've called me to be on display so anoint my every breath
Allow my tongue to bring in life and not the power of death

Rejoice

This is just a little reminder
That you always have a choice
To gripe, murmur, or complain
Or simply just
Rejoice

Some days are really difficult
With one trouble after another
And it's so easy just to dump
Our yuck on a sister or brother

But God has given a precious gift
For each of us have a voice
We have the option to shift our words
And instead of complain,
Rejoice

Just choose to worship and thank Him
Even though the answer's not clear
His promise is always to be with us
To trust Him and live above fear

Royal Priesthood

The Father truly loves us, of that there is no doubt
It's that special kind of love we cannot live without
We can love our trendy music, our house and fancy car
We can love our spouse to pieces or the candy in a jar

We can love our favorite movies and our one and only hat
We can love to watch the grandsons hit home runs when at bat
We can love our growing family and love our special friend
But all that love eventually will come to an end

There is only One with whom we really can treasure
Only One who gives to us pleasure without measure
There's only One absolute on which we can truly rely
The Heavenly Father is faithful and never does He lie

Come to Him in thankfulness for blessings by the score
Praise Him for His priceless love and all that we adore
Worship Him in relationship for He created us to be
An humble, simple sacrifice to carry His authority

We are a kingdom of priests because we believe on His Son
As priests we minister in the world to the saved and the undone
A priestly ministry is three-fold. I'm sure that you agree
As priests our ministry must include our God with intimacy

Oh, how precious is our God to place in us such trust
Of spreading His light throughout the world, it simply is a must
For darkness has invaded but it doesn't have to be
We simply need to recognize and take our authority

We are a royal priesthood and a chosen generation
We are a peculiar people living in a holy nation
God has brought us out of darkness into the glorious light
Let's be good stewards of our garden. It is our given right

A statement was made that Rome wasn't built in only a single day
Darkness has invaded our garden for years in much the same way
Becoming a sacrifice for Him prepares us to answer His call
His trust in us as ministering priests invites us to give Him our all

Choices

Inferior feelings, inferior thought

Inferior reactions is what it brought

Choices are available every day

As to what to do and what to say

Do you tell them how you really feel

Or submit yourself to the Father's will?

It's not always easy to make the right choice

For you are often hearing more than one voice

It comes down to trusting that voice from the throne

Above the enemy and that of your own

I'm not the one in charge or second in despair

You've given me the anointing to operate right there

You always have a Choice
Bitter or Better

Boiling with hate

In an agitated state

Time to be depressed

Thoughts are distressed

Everything goes wrong

Rather not sing a song

Bitter is *NEVER* better

Being in peace

Experiencing release

Time to watch and pray

Thank God for this day

Every song we sing

Rejoice and praise the King

Better is *ALWAYS* better

Hope Deferred

The Bible says that hope deferred makes the heart sick

You must decide to let it go and get over that real quick

Stop a moment and let yourself hold onto the Master's hands

Know that you need to receive God's–not the enemy's–plans

The enemy haunts you day and night just waiting for the time

When you have made a little mistake or gotten out of line

He's very good at reminding you of every faulty choice

Then he speaks clearly to you in his very negative voice

As you begin to 'should' on yourself, know that it's his thought

Failure and condemnation are the gifts that he just brought

It helps to have the Word of God hidden within your heart

Then you are prepared to answer him before he even starts

God has made a way for us where there seems to be no way

He reveals His keys for victory in the Word and when we pray

So when the enemy comes at you and deferred has been your hope

Just say, "I have talked with God and He said to tell you *Nope!*"

Encounters

Just when you think that He is not listening
Just when you think that He's just saying no
Into your life pops the strangest encounter
What you thought was dead, God causes to grow

Often we think we really did miss it
Or maybe the problem was we'd gotten too old
And when we least are expecting to hear Him
He comes across with an encounter of gold

It may be a phone call or maybe a letter
A strong impression which we can't deny
It may be a dream or an afternoon vision
God's timing is perfect while we wonder why

God makes us promises we have been called to
But it never turns out the way that we thought
For God's plan is bigger than we had imagined
And deeper than any ideas we had sought

Let's leave all the scheming to the Master of plans
Simply abide in His presence and yield
For the Master Designer has a glorious plan
To bear beautiful fruit in our designated field

It may not be like we thought it would be
His promises are true and so is His plan
For we can do nothing apart from Him
We must only abide and hold tight to His hand

Chapter 5

The Lighter Side

My ABC's

I'm looking at the alphabet. It goes from **A to Z.**
How can this simple alphabet describe someone like me?

A means I'm sometimes Angry

B means I can be crabby like a Bear

C means I can be Crafty

D means sometimes I Don't really care

E means I often Eat too much

F means I'm growing Fat

G means I often Go too much

H means I need Help with that

I means I'm very Impatient

J means I'm Jealous at times

K means I need to use Kindness

L means I Like to write rhymes

M means I am a Mother

N means I try to be Nice

O means I'm growing Older

P means I always check the Price

Q means I ask lots of Questions

R means I love to Read

S means I do a lot of Sneezing

T means I'm allergic to That weed

U means I was Under the weather

V means I felt Very bad

W means I drink lots of Water

X means many X-rays I've had

Y mens Yes, God is watching over me

Z means Zip up the negative, God has set me free

The Closet

I went to the closet to find something to wear
But to my disappointment there was nothing there

    The closet was packed and stacked to the max
    But nothing I could wear hung on the racks

The truth of the matter that I must confess
There were lots of things with which I could dress

    With deep disappointment this one fact I knew
    There was nothing to wear because nothing was new

My husband was preparing to go to a meeting
But nothing to wear in the closet did greet him

    The closet was full from the top to the floor
    In fact you could not add anything more

But the truth of the matter remains to be seen
With all of the clothes, there was nothing CLEAN

    Now it's launder for him and shopping for me
    Then we'll both be happy, I'm sure you agree

Pampering the soul had become my delight
But God said correct it and do what is right

    So I'll clean the closet and set my heart to rest
    For God says Simplicity simply is the best

The End of My But

I wanted to return your call **but** I really was too busy
I wanted to go to your party **but** my hair suddenly went frizzy

I was going to write you a letter **but** I couldn't find a pen
I wanted to go to the wedding **but** I wasn't sure where or when

I wanted to go to church with you **but** your church gets out late
I needed to go to the doctor **but** I couldn't stand the wait

I wanted to praise God with song **but** I don't sing really well
I didn't want to be late to class **but** I didn't hear the bell

I wanted to help with the dishes **but** I got to talking instead
I wanted to come and worship **but** it was nice and warm in my bed

I wanted to spend time in prayer **but** I've got so many things to do
I wanted to come and visit **but** I'm afraid that I'll catch the flu

I wanted to help you with cooking **but** I'm not a very good cook
I intended to bring you a little gift **but** I forgot to look

I told you I'd meet you at seven **but** time just slipped away
I know you have a birthday **but** I forgot the month and the day

I wanted to thank you for helping me **but** things were on my mind
I wanted to keep my bills paid **but** I found myself way behind

I planned to paint the bedroom **but** there was a catch in my hip
I wanted to wear a special dress **but** I forgot to fix the rip

Things have gone from bad to worse and it's all because of my **but**
There are so many things I want to do **but** I find myself in a rut

I've decided to have a funeral and bury this **but** for good
To do what I first intended and what I really should

You're invited to come to the funeral and see the **but** get its due
The funeral will start at one o'clock **but** it could possibly be at two

The Question Was...

DO YOU LEAVE THE CAP ON OR OFF
    AFTER BRUSHING YOUR TEETH?

To answer your question I really must say

That's a jolly good question to brighten up my day

Off comes the cap and out comes the paste

The color is green with a minty taste

I brush with vigor and rinse with a cup

Then it's time to put everything up

Carefully I place the cap on the paste

I twist it on tight so there isn't any waste

It's a very boring ritual, but I'm sure you agree

It's really worth the effort when you're talking to me

The Computer

A necessary evil has entered my house

A computer I have needed so much

To capture my thoughts as they roll through my head

And expose them with a moment's touch

For days all goes well with never a hitch

My machine is one in which I can depend

But just when I need it the very most

It no longer operates as my friend

At times in a hurry I sit down to write

As words through my brain swiftly flow

But waiting and waiting just to connect

My computer clearly says "NO!"

I try to treat it with deepest respect

With patience I work hard and long

But when success is just within reach

The printer says something's gone wrong

You can speed, you can spell, you can even indent

In so many ways you are grand

But when all else fails in the midst of my wails

I resort to the method called longhand

Has anybody seen my ink pen?

Ode to a Dryer

Dryer, dryer in my bath
Sometimes you just make me laugh
You groan and grind as if in pain
The sound you make is quite insane

Your load indeed is never light
In fact I load you FULL in spite
For all the noise that does confuse
And all the electricity that you use

I know you think you are very 'hot'
But often I find you're really not
So once again you must be started
Your drying sometimes is so half-hearted

It's in the cold winter or on a rainy day
Your loud exclamations bring me dismay
For I cannot put clothes to dry on the line
I don't have the patience, desire, or time

You're supposed to lighten, not lengthen my work
You're called a time-saver, so why do you jerk?
You clank and clunk with tennis shoes and jeans
You rumble and tumble by whatever means

And sometimes a pocket conceals a little gum
Then every piece of clothing is slathered with some
Extra heavy duty is a must with boys in sports
Night-time drying is required for uniforms and shorts

At times a certain clanging catches my ear in range
A very thoughtful person forgot to remove his pocket change
It's not much consolation, but I really choose to thank
Someone who left a quarter or dime for the piggy bank

Forgive my tendency to complain, murmur, and even grumble
For life goes on from day to day and continuous is the rumble
But one piece of wisdom I find is true without a single doubt
A dutiful dryer with living surround sound, I cannot live without

Photo courtesy of Jason Duane Luman.

Chapter 6

Beholding Beauty

Beholding Beauty

God lets me see beauty in oh so many ways
Each time that it happens, my heart gives God praise

Early one morning my car lights caught the scene
Of a beautiful, majestic buck standing proud and serene

Smoke rose from his nostrils as his head was tilted back
I gasped in surprise and wonder at the size of his rack

Fur covered his chest, thick and dark, against the bitter cold
A picture worth a thousand words and more, a pot of gold

Then early on my way to work on another special day
I caught two beautiful fawns frolicking around in play

They were prancing upon a bridge, and chasing all around
My interruption scared them and they swiftly leaped to ground

One day I saw an eagle as it soared above the trees
Gently rising higher as it caught a silent breeze

Awesome was its wingspread as it circled toward its nest
In the deep end of our pasture where it gently came to rest

Four beautiful doe in my front yard came to see
If there were any acorns left beneath our old oak tree

Two baby raccoons followed their momma across the street
As they waddled very quickly heading straight for the creek

God, thank you for our eyes and allowing us to view
The wonders of the world created just for us by You

The Hummingbird

A tiny little hummingbird gave me such a thrill
As it fluttered and it hovered at my kitchen windowsill
Luscious red tomatoes in the window caught its sight
Oblivious of my presence, it darted left and right

Then hovering oh so closely, this tiny little creation
Stood still to check out each tomato with great anticipation
It caught my breath to see its wings beating in the air
Moving so fast you'd never know that they were even there

I could see the movement of a heart within its tiny breast
And though in constant motion it appeared to be at rest
It never touched the window but inspected each color bright
Looking to find sweet nectar before it took to flight

In an instant it was gone. It vanished to who knows where
As I waited for its return, God's presence filled the air
God, thank you for this moment that took me by surprise
A glimpse of your beautiful creation that passed before my eyes

When Holy Spirit hovered in love across this land
A world of beauty was created by touch of the Master's hand
Let's not be too busy to miss those moments of revelation
Just bask in His intimate presence with joyous celebration

Road Obstruction

It was early in the morning and I was in a hurry

Didn't want to be late for work, my mind was in a flurry

I saw him in the distance slowly shuffle across the road

Taking his leisure time as if carrying a heavy load

I pumped the brake and slowed down barely to a crawl

He didn't even look at me or acknowledge my presence at all

He was indifferent to my tardiness and utter irritation

He was concerned only with himself which added to my frustration

At last he reached the other side but not even a nod I received

Good turns are surely worthy of praise, at least it's what I believed

All day long my thoughts returned to the traveler on the road

I wondered what was on his mind, just how heavy was his load?

Returning home I saw him by the side of the road racked with pain

He must have been hit by another car as he crossed the road again

His limbs were barely able to move, a slow death I could tell

Gently I turned him over lifting him carefully by his shell

He quickly drew in his arms and legs and tucked in his little head

I left that turtle but didn't know if he would live or be dead

The next day as I went to work I slowed down and looked to see

But the sight of the slow-moving creature was not observed by me

Today God told me "thank you." His heart I did surely please

Because I gave my very best to one of the least of these

A Tiny Flutter

As I sat within my bedroom
   Contemplating with quiet repose
   What did I see but a tiny hummingbird
   Sipping nectar from a bright red rose

Darting swiftly in and out
Then disappearing quick as a wink
Soon to return with wings aflutter
Stealing yet another drink

Wings so tiny moving fast
Quicker than the human eye
No time to give a sweet hello
No longer there to say goodbye

Amazing is our great Creator
Who made a creature swift in flight
To catch our eye in a moment brief
And bless us for that instant sight

Reflection

This morning I saw on the window screen
A huge Luna Moth colored beautiful green
It latched to the screen and was very still
It is early in April and the weather is chill

Perhaps it's much too early for it to come to life
The coldness of the morning has created real strife
Moisture on its wings suggest a very recent birth
Or possibly a rainy mist has fallen on the earth

I checked on it frequently throughout a busy day
I knew that a hungry bird could be its fatal prey
But God placed on its wings a lovely small surprise
Two colored spots looking like a pair of angry eyes

The morning passed so quickly and to my sheer delight
Clouds disappeared and a warm beautiful sun shone bright
Sometime in the afternoon the moth was no longer there
Was it alive or did it die? I have no knowledge to share

It caused me to reflect upon how swiftly fly my days
My time on earth is very brief in oh so many ways
I reflect and then I regret and just end up by crying
Too late to change a single thing, for eventually we're dying

How Do You?

How do you measure the impact of a raindrop upon a plant?
How do you fathom the weight of a grain carried by an ant?
How can you create the pleasure of the song of many birds?
How can you measure the depth of a portion of God's words?

How can you capture the smell of a rosebud about to bloom?
How can you describe the essence of a gentle waft of perfume?
How can you describe the emotion of a mother's first tender smile?
As she snuggles her newborn baby when it nurses a little while?

The laughter of little children as they giggle and laugh at play
Is as hard to describe as the sunset we see at the end of the day
The height of majestic mountains or slope of a snow-packed trail
Are beyond our finest description and words just seem to fail

It's because we are the creation and the Creator wants to show
It's beyond our comprehension and just for Him to know
Because the Father loves us so He created for our pleasure
A world of sound and color for enjoyment without measure

So we don't have to understand, describe, or even measure
We only need to talk to Him. Our intimacy brings Him pleasure
A thankful heart of love in prayer we simply to Him lift
With praise and honor worship Him for each and every gift

Winter Surprise

Looking out the window one winter morn, the sky cloudy and gray
The scene was dull and very drab after the snow had melted away
Thoughts of spring could not come with brown before my eyes
But when I looked at the Redbud tree in our yard, I saw a surprise

The Redbud tree had lost its leaves in the fall but retained its seeds
There they hung in huge dark clumps like bunches of ugly weeds
What caught my eye was the brilliant red of Cardinals resting there
Five of them perched like bright red bulbs shining in the crispy air

Fluffy and round with feathers and a beak orange and bright
Resting a moment while watching, then instantly taking flight
Creation's beauty surrounds us, Lord. Open my eyes – let me see
Let me bask in wonders of beauty which You have created for me

Tears filled my eyes as I feasted on such a beautiful scene
As I looked the dull and drab disappeared. My mind became serene
Courage and hope rose in my heart for promises made in the Word
Spring will arrive with color again like wings of a beautiful bird.

Photo courtesy of Jason Duane Luman.

www.ingramcontent.com/pod-product-compliance
Lightning Source LLC
Chambersburg PA
CBHW060518300426
44112CB00017B/2717

9 780976 432555